ALL SANTIAGO

editorial **escudo de oro, s.a.** Palaudarias, 26 - 08004 Barcelona - Spain

Panorama of Compostela in an old engraving.

THE MEMORY OF THE APOSTLE, GUIDING LIGHT OF THE WEST

Santiago stands on a small rise at a height of approximately 260 m above sea-level; from this privileged site the city enjoys splendid panoramas of the Sar and Sarela valleys spread out poetically at its feet. The fertile countryside — a marvellous symphony in green — embraces the urban area with, as it were, loving humility; and it extends clearly as far as the rugged landscapes of central and northern Galicia, while to the south it stretches gently towards the paradisiacal *Rías Bajas* ("Lower Estuaries").

In the words of Otero Pedrayo, Santiago is "the most modern city in Galicia and the most recent of all the religious and cultural metropolises in Europe. Like Venice, it has no ancient history. Its transition from prehistory and the anonymity of its fields and forests to a place in history was direct, and the result of the miracle. The 'invention' of the Apostle's tomb took place during the reign of Alfonso II *el Casto* ("the Chaste"), between 812 and 814 AD, i.e. shortly after Charlemagne's coronation at S Peter's in Rome.''

It seems, however, that as early as the 1st century (precisely when the Apostle James arrived in the Iberian peninsula) or the 2nd, Compostela (*campus stellae* or "field of stars" for some, *Campus Apostoli* or, again, *Compositum* for others) was a Roman site and previously, perhaps, a Celtic settlement. Having completed his evangelical mission in the lands of Iberia, Jacobus was decapitated in Jerusalem (in the year 44) and his embalmed remains were transported from the port of Joppa (now Jaffa) to Iria-Flavia, where they were buried; the discovery of the tomb in

A group of statues depicting the Apostle on his legendary white horse, attacking unbelievers.

A charming picture of the beautiful Plaza de las Platerías.

The popular Fuente de los Caballos *and the "Dean's House."*

the early 9th century was to give rise to the foundation of Santiago de Compostela (*Santiago* - Spanish for James). The city soon became an important landmark for mediaeval Christianity and zealous pilgrims flocked to it from all corners of the western world. Compostela's early history is intimately associated with the evolution of these pilgrimages to S James' tomb and with the development of Romanesque art. When Alfonso II heard about the discovery of the Apostle's tomb, he had a small church built on the site (its original name was *Arca Marmórica* and it was surrounded by hill-forts and necropolises dating back, perhaps, to the Celts); this was the first church raised in honour of S James and was later to be replaced by one of the most beautiful and impressive cathedrals in

the whole world. We should, however, record that there are many authors who state that the remains lying in the tomb at Santiago de Compostela are those, not of S James, but of Priscilian, the interesting Galician heresiarch who was burned alive at Treier at the end of the 4th century.

In its early history Compostela was, as Otero Pedrayo noted, "a group of monasteries, a centre for hermits, as at Thebes," until, after the battle of Clavijo, the Apostle — the mythical "Son of Thunder" — became the patron saint of Hispanic Christianity. From this moment onwards the city began to be one of the most prestigious and dynamic dioceses in the western world; and this brilliant rôle was not checked by the vicissitudes which befell the city, such as the

A graceful view of the Azabachería façade.

bloody incursions of the Vikings in the 9th century and of Almanzor in the 10th. After its destruction by Almanzor on August 11th, 997, the city was rebuilt by the bishop who presided over the See of Santiago de Compostela at that time, San Pedro de Mezonzo, who is thought to have been the author of the *Salve Regina,* one of the most beautiful prayers used by Catholics. Otero Pedrayo writes that "the Africans destroyed everything except the tomb of the Apostle; an aged monk — according to Don Rodrigo Jiménez de Rada, the only inhabitant of the city present when the enemy approached — was praying by its side: he adds that Almanzor spared the old man's life."

Two centuries later the genius of Bishop Gelmírez made of Santiago — by then promoted to arch-diocese — a vigorous cultural and religious centre whose splendid spiritual illumination influenced all the western world. The structure of Compostela began to acquire a characteristic Romanesque personality and its outdated mediaeval appearance was gradually converted into the beautiful, unmistakable city-cum-monument that dazzles both natives and strangers nowadays.

After the discovery — or "invention" — of the Apos-tle's tomb, a multitude of churches was built in honour of S James, not only in Spain but throughout western Europe. When the Christian world learned the news of the discovery of S James' tomb, the first

Magnificent close-up of the Romanesque porticoed doors of Platerías.

pilgrimages to Compostela were organized. They increased and took on a universal nature when, in 1181, Alexander III published the *Regis Eterni* Bull, granting plenary indulgence and the remission of sins to all penitent pilgrims. If the pilgrimage was undertaken in a Holy Year (i.e. when July 25th, S James' day, falls on a Sunday), the remission of sins was extended to those whose forgiveness had been reserved by the Holy See. The Holy Year was instituted by Pope Callisto II — uncle of Alfonso VII, king of Galicia — and this privilege was later ratified by Eugene II, Anastasius IV and Alexander II. Its celebration greatly intensified pilgrimages from all over Europe to Compostela throughout the Middle Ages. The pilgrims'

road to Santiago became a universal route and Compostela was converted into a spiritual beacon for the Christian world.

There were two routes through France for pilgrims from Europe on their way to Santiago to gain indulgence. One route began at Saint-Martin in Tours, Sainte-Madeleine in Vézelay, and Notre-Dame du Puy, continuing respectively via the churches of Saint-Hilaire in Poitiers, Saint-Jean-d'Angély and Saint-Eutrope in Saintes; via Saint-Léonard and Saint-Front in Périgueux; and Sainte-Foy in Conques and Saint-Pierre in Moissac. The pilgrims converged in Aquitaine and entered Spain by the Roncesvalles pass.

Close-up of the splendid Pórtico de la Gloria.

The Puerta Santa ("Holy Door"), giving onto the Quintana de los Muertos.

The characteristic silhouette of the clock-tower. ▷

Pilgrimages from the South of France, on the other hand, passed through Saint-Gilles, Montpellier and Toulouse, crossing into Spanish territory at Canfranc. Once in Spain, the pilgrims from the other side of the Pyrenees joined up with Spaniards also on their way to prostrate themselves before the tomb of S James; the motley pilgrimages followed the pilgrims' road via Puente de la Reina, Estella, Logroño, Nájera, Santo Domingo de la Calzada, Burgos, Frómista, Carrión de los Condes, Sahagún, León, El Puente Orbigo del Paso Honroso, Astorga and Ponferrada, entering Galicia through the rugged mountains of El Cebrero (the scene of the Galician version of the miracle of the Holy Grail). They continued through Triacastela, Samos, Portomarín (a Romanesque town whose original site on the banks of the Miño has been covered by the water of a reservoir), Melide and, approaching Santiago, Labacolla (where the airport is now).

On arrival in Compostela, the pilgrims inundated the

The coffer containing S James' relics, kept in the Crypt.

city streets with fervour and cosmopolitanism. The Christian spirit of the West transformed Santiago, giving it an atmosphere of universality: a permanent spiritual destination, not a place of anecdotal passage. The metropolis of S James received and assimilated the flood of pilgrims that poured in, and was in turn enriched in human and cultural terms: the pilgrimages from Europe gave rise to a splendid flourishing of the arts in the Apostle's city. Otero Pedrayo wrote that "the genius and art of Santiago would be incomprehensible were it not for Compostela's, and Galicia's, contact and communication with Europe, especially with Burgundy and Lorraine."

Not only the magic of Romanesque stone architecture — so gloriously represented in Compostela — but also the marvellous poetry of the *cancioneros* (verse anthologies) are closely associated with the mediaeval phenomenon of the pilgrimages that arrived in the Galician city by the road to Santiago. Airas Nunes, a 13th-century poet and cleric from Santiago, proclaimed in beautiful verses the high breeding of no few pilgrims:

> *A Santiago en romería ven*
> *El Rei, madre, e prázeme de coraçón*
> *por duas cousas, se Deus me perdón,*

The Puerta Santa, *also called* Puerta de los Perdones, *seen from the interior.*

Compostela Cathedral: the Quintana façade.

Main front of the cathedral, facing the Plaza del Obradoiro. ▷

en que teño que me faz Deus gran ben:
ca verei El Rei, que nunca vi,
e meu amigo, que ven con él í.

Another mediaeval poet, Ayras Corpancho, reflected the fervour of the pilgrims to Santiago in that period:

Por facer romería puxe én meu coraçón
a Sant-Yago un día, por facer oraçón
e por veer meu amigo logo í.

The pilgrimages to Compostela were made up of people of all social classes, from kings, princes and bishops to persons of the humblest standing,

mystics, anonymous saints, rogues, cardsharpers, beggars, adventurers, mendicants, poets... Of the most illustrious pilgrims, those generally mentioned are S Evermero (Bishop of Friesland), S Francis of Assisi, Santo Domingo de Guzmán, S Louis, San Vicente Ferrer, Santa Isabel of Portugal...

Bishop Gelmírez succeeded in having Alfonso VII crowned in Santiago, had several confrontations with Doña Urraca, and was persecuted by the people of Santiago in the uprising of 1117, when his brother Gudesindo and other personages allied with the battling prelate were killed. Like him, Bishops Pedro Gudesteiz and Pedro Suárez de Deza later gave constant, considerable impetus to the building works of

An aspect of the fine Pórtico de la Gloria.

the cathedral, which was consecrated in the early 13th century.

In the following century, however, there were bitter struggles between the inhabitants of Compostela and the Frenchman Berenguel de Landore, who was appointed Archbishop of Santiago; this prelate even ordered the massacre of the emissaries that the authorities of Santiago had sent to La Rocha castle to negotiate with him. Also in the 14th century (29th July, 1336), Don Pedro "the Cruel" had Bishop Suero Gómez de Toledo and Dean Pedro Alvarez murdered in Santiago.

The city of the Apostle was conquered by King Fernando I of Portugal in 1370, and in 1386 it was occupied by the Duke of Lancaster: with his wife Constance, he lodged in the monastery of San Martín Pinario, intending to set up his court there. The people of Compostela, however, were not long in ejecting him from the city.

Later, the Fonsecas (there were three bishops with this surname) made a considerable contribution to Santiago's development, building numerous monuments that embellished the city. Architectural works of the importance of the Platerías façade and the cloister in the cathedral, the beautiful façade of the Hospital and the elegant courtyard of the Fonseca mansion are due to them.

In the 16th, 17th and 18th centuries the structure of the city and its spiritual character were developed in peace. Internal strife had ceased, as also threats from abroad, although in 1589 Santiago had a period of alarm as a result of the prospect of being invaded by the troops of an English fleet that was marauding off the coast of Galicia.

French troops under the command of Ney and Soult occupied the city during the War of Independence, lodging part of their forces in the cathedral cloisters; but the Galician troops commanded by Don Martín de la Carrara succeeded in recapturing Compostela shortly after.

During the 19th century Santiago became the centre

The statue of the Apostle appearing on the column of the mullion.

The charming statue of the ''santo dos croques.''

The statues on the right-hand side of the Pórtico de la Gloria.

of the different revolutionary currents that occurred in the lands of Galicia; this did not, however, make the city lose its character as a source of spiritual illumination for the West and as the religious and cultural capital of Galicia. In 1846 the revolt in favour of the Infante Don Enrique took on a nationalist character in Galicia; a revolutionary junta was even set up in Santiago, presided over by Antolín Faraldo. The military coup was unsuccessful and its leaders were executed by firing squad in Carral.

Ten years earlier, the law dispossessing the clergy of their goods, promulgated by Mendizábal, had had a significant social effect in Santiago since it caused many monks of different religious orders to vacate the monasteries that had belonged to their communities and housed their members for centuries.

Another event of indubitable importance in the 19th-century history of Santiago was the famous banquet held in Conxo woods on March 2nd, 1856: this celebration was organized by Aurelio Aguirre (a poet who was soon after to be drowned in La Coruña), Eduardo Pondal (forming, with Rosalía de Castro and Curros Enríquez, the trio of most important poets in the *rexurdimento* — Renaissance — of Galician literature) and Rodríguez Seoane. Workers and students were present at the banquet, poems were read in Galician, the distinct personality of Galicia was defended, and there were toasts to freedom.

The subtle, momentous spirit of Compostela is reflected today in the verses by García-Bodaño:

Compostela é unha rúa longa
na memoria
onde vagan os nomes
e as horas
que cada quen recorda...
Tempo de eternidade nas sombras
case vougas
a caír polos días
e as cousas
maino como unha choiva.

The cathedral's impressive interior glimpsed from the Pórtico de la Gloria.

The majestic interior of this superlative church in Santiago, sketched behind the filigreed stone of the Pórtico de la Gloria.

A view of the cathedral's high altar.

The lavishly-adorned image of the Apostle James that stands on the high altar.

The cathedral's main front dominates the skyline of Compostela.

The statue of the Apostle atop the Puerta Santa; the enchanting image of David adorning the Pórtico de la Gloria (pages 24/25).

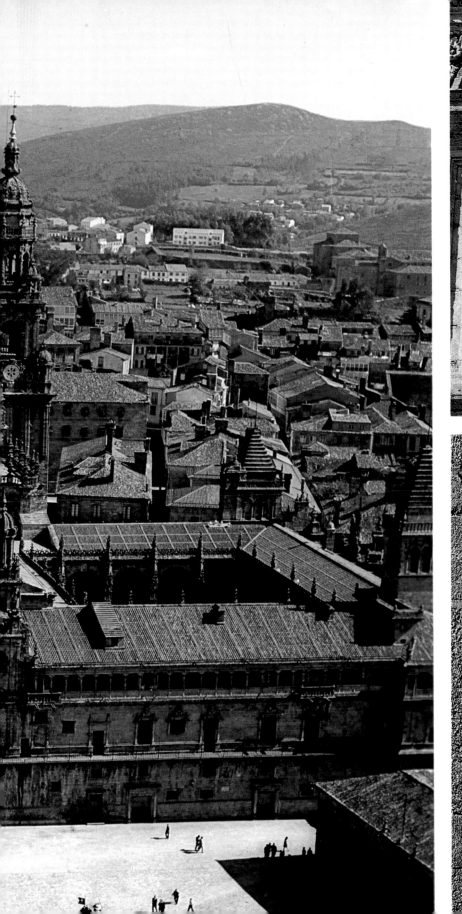

The
beautiful
Gothic
screen at the
entrance to
the artistic
Mondragón
chapel.

The marvellous Pórtico de la Gloria, *an unsurpassed jewel of* Romanesque Compostela.

A splendid view of the interior, emphasizing the baroque magnificence of the high altar.

El Salvador chapel.

Altar of the "Virgen de la Soledad."

THE CATHEDRAL

The first basilica at Compostela was built during the reign of Alfonso II *el Casto,* in the early 9th century; the second (in Pre-Romanesque style, destroyed by Almanzor), during the reign of Alfonso III *el Magno* ("the Great"), at the end of the same century. The present-day cathedral was raised on the ruins of the second basilica: the building works began around 1075, when Alfonso VI was on the throne and the See of Santiago was occupied by Diego Peláez. The altars were consecrated about 1105, and the church was practically complete by 1122. The beautiful Platerías façade was inaugurated in 1103 and the marvellous Romanesque ensemble of the *Pórtico de la Gloria* was finished twenty-five years later. With the construction of the Azabachería façade (concluded in the middle of the 18th century), Santiago basilica presented essentially its present-day architectural appearance. Ogival, baroque and plateresque additions gradually obscured the original church (pure Romanesque in style) over the centuries. The baroque façade — now the main front — giving onto the Plaza del Obradoiro was built between 1738 and 1750; this square is an architecturally admirable framework for it, full of majesty, successfully harmonising art and nature. The

An angle of the cathedral's Tapestries Museum, which
has exhibits of considerable value: the most outstanding
are the twelve tapestries based on cartoons by Goya,
produced at the Royal Workshop in Madrid and donated
by Canon Don Pedro de Acuña in the early 19th century.

A handsome shot of the Chapter Hall; the ceiling is decorated with chiaroscuro and blue frescoes by Ferro Caaveiro.

Magnificent, enormous brazier, decorated with pilgrims' symbolical scallop-shells.

cathedral spires and the lush greenery of the countryside that may be seen from them dominate the magnificent square's topography and constitute two aesthetic divisions inseparably joined in the spirit of Compostela.

Many craftsmen intervened in the realization of this stone masterpiece that is the cathedral of Santiago de Compostela; but none can compare, in terms of creative genius, with the legendary *maestro* Mateo, to whose glorious authorship the *Pórtico de la Gloria* is attributed, for this is undoubtedly the most precious jewel of all Romanesque art.

The main front of the church stands opposite the *Palacio* ("mansion") *de Rajoy.* The *Hostal de los*

Reyes Católicos ("Hotel of the Catholic Monarchs") is to the right of the beautiful, spacious Plaza del Obradoiro; on the left-hand side, the ancient *Colegio de San Jerónimo* displays a fine Romanesque doorway. This cathedral front facing the Plaza del Obradoiro is made up of a raised triptych above a broad stairway divided into two parts, with the door of the crypt or old cathedral between them. Two graceful towers with balconies crown the lateral sections of the central triptych, which is scored with windows, arches and niches. This façade of the cathedral is a filigreed work of ornamentation and here and there it displays artistic flourishes, scrolls, tympana and obelisks. A statue of the Apostle in pilgrim's

A beautiful carving of the "Virgen de la Esperanza."

The superb gilt silver monstrance made by Arfe, one of the most precious pieces in the Cathedral Treasure.

Pieces from the Cathedral Treasure: chalice, paten and pitchers.

A dazzling close-up of the "Reliquias" chapel.

dress stands on the topmost arch. The decorative sculptures are in the baroque style.

The highly popularised architectural image of this monumental Obradoiro façade is topped by two slender, lordly towers, named *de las Campanas* ("bell-tower") and *de la Carraca.* Viewed from the Rajoy mansion, the façade (built from 1738 to 1750) is impressive for its grandiosity and for its bold baroque lines, which nowhere lose their agile majesty. This is one of the most successful examples of baroque architecture and constitutes an unmistakably Compostelan image.

After putting this monumental façade behind him by entering the cathedral, the visitor finds himself before the *Pórtico de la Gloria:* a miracle in stone. The sensa-

tion of surprise and admiration upon contemplating the indescribable beauty of this unique work of art is overwhelming. The superb porch comprises three arches, corresponding to the nave and two nave-aisles inside the church, with a pillar dividing the centre arch into two apertures. The centre of the tympanum is occupied by a large statue of Jesus, worked with splendid artistry, showing the wounds in His side and feet; this statue gives a subtle order to the extraordinary architectural composition. One has the sensation of being before a perfect work of art. Although overwhelmed with wonder, at the same time one has the impression of contemplating a prodigy of simplicity; simplicity imbued, *par excellence,* with the magic of art.

Compostela Cathedral: the popular botafumeiro, *or censer.*

The central figure of Christ is surrounded by statues: S John on an eagle, S Luke on a bull, S Mark on a lion and S Matthew kneeling. Below, on the base of the tympanum, figure eight angels holding the following instruments of the Passion: the whipping-post, cross, crown of thorns, nails, spear, the parchment with Christ's sentence, the scourges, reed and sponge.

The whole group of statues is executed with insuperable mastery. The poetical talent of the master craftsman, Mateo, shines through the stone: it seems to vibrate spiritually and substantially, as though the carved figures were, in fact, of flesh and blood. At the base of the pillar, or mullion (made up of several columns joined by the capital) that divides the centre arch, there is a monstrous carving; behind it, facing the altar, one may see a kneeling figure. This is said to depict the *maestro* Mateo himself and it is popularly known as *O santo dos croques* — the saint of bumps on the head: the general public honours it by knocking their heads against it because legend has it that the talent of this genial artist is contagious.

It is impossible to describe the beauty of this pinnacle of the Romanesque style. To gaze on it is an ecstatic pleasure, one's spirit is inundated with mediaeval resonance and artistic images of the oldest, purest kind.

The vaults and pillars of the crypt or old cathedral are below the *Pórtico de la Gloria:* this seems to have been the site of the original basilica and has the shape

A view of the Puerta Real ("Royal Door").

Magnificent close-up of the ogive vaults in the cathedral cloister, one of the largest in Spain.

Magnificent close-up of the lordly façade of the Chapter House — considered to be the crowning work of the baroque style in Compostela — in the Plaza de las Platerías (pages 40/41).

Part of the cathedral and the Palacio de Gelmírez.

of a Latin cross, divided into two aisles by three pillars.

In the Plaza de las Platerías, surrounded by fine buildings and with the Los Caballos ("Horses") fountain in the middle, there is the only surviving façade of the cathedral's original exterior. The portico, in an enchanting Romanesque style, is profusely adorned. The basic structure and several of the statues date from the last quarter of the 11th century. This is a double portico; of the artistic decoration displayed on the arches, we should highlight the extraordinarily fine sculptures depicting the woman taken in adultery — kissing the skull of her lover, which she has in her lap —, Jesus miraculously curing a blind man,

Abraham praying, David playing the viol, and a woman sitting on a lion and suckling a child. An excellent depiction of the Apostle stands above the arches.

The *Puerta Santa* ("Holy Door," also called the Door of Pardons, to which the public only has access in jubilee years) is orientated towards the Quintana de los Muertos and supports twelve Romanesque statues on each side. It is crowned by a group of sculptures made up of the Apostle, in pilgrim's dress, and his disciples Athanasius and Theodore at his side. The Azabachería façade gives onto the square of the same name, which in the Middle Ages was called "Paradise" and was the part of the city where the

European pilgrims' road to S James' tomb finished. The pilgrims changed money in the Plaza de la Azabachería — where the guild of money-changers was based — and bought diverse articles there. The façade that we see today dates from the middle of the 18th century. It was designed by Ferro Caaveiro and Fernández Sarela, Ventura Rodríguez and Lois Montenegro intervened in its construction.

The cathedral church measures about 100 m long in the nave by 70 m in the transept; these dimensions are 97 m and 65 m, respectively, inside. The imposing monument occupies an area of approximately 23,000 square metres. This is, then, not only one of the most original, most beautiful cathedrals in the world, but also one of the largest. The ensemble is of incalculable artistic and historical value; its unique structure combines styles as widely contrasted as Romanesque, Gothic, plateresque and Baroque in a surprising architectural synthesis.

The cathedral's interior structure is of Romanesque characteristics, with ground-plan in the shape of a Latin cross, nave and two nave-aisles in the main body of the church, transept, triforium, round arches and apse aisle; barrel vaulting in the centre, cross vaults at the sides. With respect to the interior, which is very richly ornamented, special mention should be made of the lavish chancel, which stands over the crypt where the Apostle's remains were buried (they

Façade of the Universidad Literaria.

The Hostal de los Reyes Católicos *seen from the cathedral; the sumptuous* Salón Real *and one of the luxurious hotel rooms.*

Superb close-up of the artistic plateresque front of the
Hostal de los Reyes Católicos, *in the impressive Plaza del*
Obradoiro, by the cathedral and the old Palacio de Rajoy,
now the seat of Compostela's civic authorities.

*Various aspects of typical streets in Santiago: always a
fascinating human spectacle, with their original,
unmistakable physiognomy.*

were hidden due to the prospect of invasion by the
English in the 16th century, and only rediscovered in
1879); the chancel is at the intersection of the centre
nave and the apse aisle. The granite columns of the
original Romanesque fabric are now obscured by
jasper and marble pedestals and opulent baroque ornamentation. The high altar, with silver fittings, dates
from the late 17th century and was altered at the end
of the 19th. The precious, early 18th-century Taber-
nacle is particularly attractive. In the rear of the
chancel is a baroque niche with a seated image of S
James, a Romanesque carving in polychrome stone,
lit by a lamp that was a gift from Gonzalo Fernández
de Córdoba —the *Gran Capitán*— and by four
candles commemorating the battle of El Salado. The
whole of the chancel is richly adorned; the carvings
depicting S James on the pulpits are outstanding.

The popular Rúa del Villar with its characteristic colonnades, and the cathedral outlined in the background.

Rain is a familiar element in the city.

The five chapels in the apse, opening off the elegant apse aisle that encloses the high altar, are also very notable: El Pilar chapel has a very attractive, profusely decorated octagonal cupola and is an exemplary specimen of the sumptuous Galician Baroque style; Mondragón chapel, dating from the 16th century, has artistic bossed vaulting and an elegant Gothic balcony. The chapel of *Nuestra Señora de la Azucena* (Madonna of the Lilies) displays Romanesque lines and, in the apse, a baroque reredos; while that of El Salvador (The Saviour), which was bestowed by Charles V of France, has barrel vaults and artistic capitals supporting the round vault of the apse, with a beautiful plateresque reredos by Juan de Alava. The fifth chapel is in a beautiful Romanesque style and dedicated to S Bartholomew.

The chapel of *Reliquias* (Relics) is similarly of great interest: it is reached via an artistic plateresque doorway in the Epistle side aisle. The chapel was built by Juan de Alava in 1527 and displays a splendid stellar vault. The invaluable Cathedral Treasure is housed here and in San Fernando chapel: among other valuable pieces, it comprises two statues of S James (14th- and 15th- centuries) the images of the Apostles from Lope de Mendoza's oratory (mid-15th-century), numerous gold and silver crucifixes (11th-, 12th-, 15th- and 17th-centuries), Antonio de Arfe's processional monstrance (1.37 m high), various lamps in different styles and a splendid collection of reliquaries, including the outstandingly rich bust of Santiago Alfeo.

Special mention must be made of La Corticela, an

Rúa Nueva, a typical street.

oratory founded in the 9th century which later belonged to the Benedictine monks of San Martín Pinario. This is a small, charming church with a superb Romanesque archway and a fine 15th-century polychrome granite statue of Christ in the Garden of Olives.

The Archives, which can be reached from the cloister, conserve the very precious Codex of Callisto, monastical records containing invaluable documentation concerning the 9th-14th centuries, the manuscripts of the *Historia Compostelana* ("History of Compostela"), a 15th-century breviary and diverse mediaeval diplomas and letters patent.

The Cathedral Museums merit a paragraph to themselves. The Library of the Chapter conserves a considerable collection of incunabula and, in one cor-

ner, the well-known form of the *botafumeiro* or censer. In the *Sala Capitular* (Chapter Hall) and the *Museo de Tapices* (Tapestries Museum) there are some magnificent tapestries based on cartoons by Teniers, Rubens and Goya. The Archaeological Museum, finally, offers a splendid collection of statues, capitals, columns, high reliefs and other meritorious pieces from the previous exterior of the 12th-century Romanesque cathedral. Certain magnificent carvings by the *maestro* Mateo and by anonymous 13th- and 14th-century sculptors are particularly otustanding; the visitor's attention is powerfully drawn to a polychrome granite image which depicts, according to some sources, S James the Great, or in the opinion of other researchers, Alfonso II *el Casto.*

One of the galleries of the Museo do Pobo Galego.

MUSEO DO POBO GALEGO

The Museum of the Galician People, installed in the galleries of the former Dominican monastery, originated as a result of the initiative of the professional association of architects of Galicia: on December 19th, 1975, this organism made a public call to various Galician individuals and institutions with the aim of promoting the organization of an ethnographical museum of Galicia. A study meeting was held in Santiago on January 24th, 1976: in response to the aforementioned call, the representatives of twelve institutions and a group of personages connected with different sectors of Galician culture participated, and it was agreed to set up the *Museo do Pobo Galego.* At a second meeting held later the same year — on April 24th — the articles

regulating the activities of the Museum's *Patronato* (board of trustees) were voted; it was officially instituted a week later.

The Museum of the Galician People now has an interesting stock, divided into different departments. Paraethnographic matters are dealt with in the sections on geographical environment, physical anthropology and historical ethnography. The department concerning the exploitation of resources includes sections dealing with agricultural ecosystems (different kinds of farms and their organization, ways of enclosing them, crops, irrigation, as well as the exploitation of woodland and upland, implements and machines for working the land, ox-carts and vehicles for the transport of people, work in the fields and farmhouses, cattle-raising activities and the corresponding implements); and also marine

Various aspects of the Museo do Pobo Galego: *its interesting ethnographic collections are installed in the former Santo Domingo monastery.*

ecosystems, with the different types of fishing vessels — *dorna, gamela* and others — and river-boats, as well as the variety of tackle for sea- and river-fishing and the capture of shellfish. The section on trades and popular art bears on weavers, carpenters, blacksmiths, *zoqueiros,* tinkers, basket-makers, umbrella-makers, and stonemasons; and on wayside stone crosses, decoration and carving. There are departments of architecture and habitat (the rural house and its outhouses, *hórreos* — the typical Galician raised granaries —, mills and bridges); of music and dances (instruments like the mediaeval hurdy-gurdy, the Jew's-harp, bagpipes and tambourine; local costumes for *fiestas* and weddings, and jewellery); and of popular literature, anthropology, superstitions, witchcraft, common law and popular medicine. Finally, the Museum has services of documentation/bibliography and restoration/conservation.

Three new rooms were opened on July 25th, 1978; one devoted to marine matters and two to popular Galician trades. In 1978 the *Museo do Pobo Galego* housed the following specialised exhibitions: stone crosses in A Estrada, Galician sun-dials, the prehistory of Galicia and the *dorna* or typical Galician fishing-boat with a single mast and lateen sail. The exhibitions held in the Museum's rooms are generally made up of material collected by members and collaborators and are sometimes accompanied by lectures and discussion groups on the particular subject. In 1979 the Museum also presented several interesting specialised exhibitions and organized a conference on the Naval History of the North-West (with the participation of Portuguese experts); and assisted in the conference on Galician Archaeology and Prehistory organized by the Padre Sarmiento Institute of Galician Studies.

The Museum of the Galician People has a library devoted mainly to Galician studies; and is responsible for a laudable task in researching and collecting material intended for new galleries.

Façade of the church at San Francisco monastery, located at one end of the street of the same name, near Asorey's monument to the Saint of Assisi; a view of the Monastery of San Lorenzo de Trasouto.

SAN FRANCISCO DE VALDEDIOS

The monastery and church of San Francisco stand at the end of the street of the same name, near the monument to the Saint, carved by Asorey. In the entrance lodge there is a plaque recording the foundation of the monastery, it states that S Francis went to visit the Apostle James and ''he was put up by a poor coalman called Cotolay, whose house was by San Payo hermitage at the foot of Pedroso hill. From there the saint went out to the hillside to spend the nights in prayer. There God revealed to him that it was His will that a monastery should be raised in the place where it is now, called *Val de Dios y Val del Infierno* ('Valley of God and of Hell')...'' According to the inscription, the coalman Cotolay, led by God, ''found a great treasure with which he built this monastery. God blessed Cotolay's house: he made a noble marriage. He was alderman of this city and built its walls that now run by San Francisco and previously went past La Azabachería. His wife is buried in La Quintana and Cotolay, the founder of this house, in this tomb that he chose for himself. He died a saintly death in the year of Our Lord 1238.''

The only surviving remnants of the original Gothic building are the five arches in the north wall of the main patio. In 1520 Parliament met in the old Chapter Hall, presided over by Charles I.

The monastery has two artistic Doric cloisters and a valuable Franciscan library. There is a magnificent statue of S Francis, carved in granite by the sculptor Ferreiro, in the façade of the church.

SAN LORENZO DE TRASOUTO

This monastery was founded in the 13th century and later passed into the control of Valdediós monastery. The church porch and some other fragments are the only vestiges of the original Romanesque building. A reredos of marble and porphyry and the white marble statues are the outstanding items in the present-day edifice.

The Students' Residence, seen from the Alameda.

SANTO DOMINGO DE BONAVAL

This monastery was associated with the Order of Preachers (Dominicans) and is now the seat of the *Museo do Pobo Galego.* It seems that Santo Domingo de Guzmán made two pilgrimages to Compostela, once at the end of the 12th century and again in 1220; he founded a Dominican community in the city of the Apostle.

Santo Domingo church is one of the largest in Santiago. It has the ground-plan of a basilica, with nave, two nave-aisles and three apses; the arches display Romanesque and Gothic decoration. The church's overall architectural effect corresponds to the canons of a transition Romanesque/Gothic style.

The façade of the monastery is in the baroque style, as is that of the church. The two buildings combine to make up a fascinating area of monuments; the majestic ensemble stands on a slope leading to a hillock from the top of which one may enjoy a fine view of the city, dotted with old houses and enchanting, half-abandoned gardens.

The 17th-century cloister, designed by Leonel de Avalle, is of great interest; stone statues and other remains of considerable architectural value may now be admired there. From one corner of the cloister the visitor can reach the curious spiral staircase (built by Domingo de Andrade, who also designed the monastery's baroque façade) that leads to a strategically-placed view-point dominating a broad, beautiful panorama of Compostela. Santo Domingo and its environs constitute one of the most characteristic and attractive areas of the many that may be visited in the city. In her book entitled *Follas Novas,* Rosalía de Castro dedicated moving verses to this church:

Santo Domingo, en onde cant'eu quixen descansa;
vidas d'a miña vida, anacos d'as entrañas.
E vos tamén, sombrisas paredes solitarias

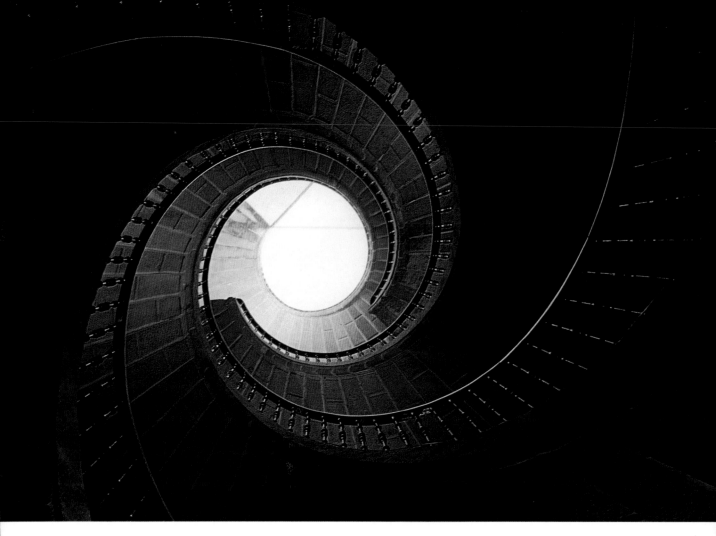

Santo Domingo church: the spiral staircase.

Santo Domingo de Bonaval: the baroque façade of the church.

que me viches chorare soia e desventurada:
¡adios!, sombras queridas, ¡adios!, sombras odiadas;
outra vez os vaivéns d'a fertuna
pra lonxe m'arrastran.

The remains of this genius, who initiated the revival of the Galician lyric tradition, lie, indeed, inside the church of Santo Domingo. The tombs of Alfredo Brañas, Asorey the sculptor and Ramón Cabanillas the poet are also in the pantheon of illustrious Galicians. Continuing up Santo Domingo slope, the visitor will encounter a cemetery whose derelict condition gives it a fascinating, romantic atmosphere; it is reached via the fine 14th-century Bonaval porch (previously a door to the monastery) with, in the tym-

panum, an image of the Virgin associated with the legend of Juan Tuorum.

Behind Santo Domingo monastery, on the other side to the Bonaval cemetery (also called *del Rosario*), is the splendid *carballeira* or oak grove of the same name, where a popular festival is held — with a meal in the open air — on July 25th, S James' Day and the *Dia da Patria Galega* (Day of Galicia). The old Callejón de Caramoniña was near the oak grove; a wily cleric, of the shrewd Galician breed who "know a trick or two," lived here: he trapped sparrows and painted them yellow so as to sell them as genuine canaries. The owner of the "Hostal Suso," one of the most attractive, popular personalities in the history of Santiago, also lived here.

San Martín Pinario church: baroque front.

SAN MARTIN PINARIO

This church is situated in the square of the same name. The ensemble of the church and the monastery constitutes the second-largest religious monument in Santiago, after the cathedral, occupying a surface area of approximately 20,000 square metres. The monastery, in the baroque style, is a spacious edifice: the main front measures some 100 m in length and is flanked by two sections standing out in the form of towers. The beautiful gallery, large windows, the entrance staircase and the façade (with an equestrian statue of San Martín Pinario) are of particular interest.

The original church was consecrated by Gelmírez in the early 12th century. The present-day edifice was built in the 17th century by Peña de Toro, Melchor de Velasco and Domingo de Andrade; the vast barrel vaulting is very eye-catching. The baroque high altar and the lower choir-stalls are very interesting.

◁ *The cathedral spires dominate the city.*

The arches, columns and vaults of Santa María la Real del Sar are curiously slanted.

The University's America Library: baroque shelves.

SANTA MARIA LA REAL DEL SAR

Santa María Collegiate Church is one of the most beautiful, original monuments in Compostela, situated "on the shores of the Sar" — *En las orillas del Sar,* the title of Rosalía de Castro's famous book of poems in Castilian. The original church was founded in the 12th century by Canon Munio Alonso (who was one of the compilers of the famous *Historia Compostelana,* and later Bishop of Mondoñedo), consecrated by Gelmírez in 1136 and confirmed by Alfonso VII the year after. The church we see today was built at the time of Pedro Gudesteiz, who occupied the archbishop's See from 1168 to 1172. Otero Pedrayo wrote that "it was a leper colony, built by Don Bernardo, the archbishop who withdrew to this monastery and is buried inside it." Monastic life declined from the 16th century onwards and Santa María la Real del Sar became a collegiate church, until in the mid-19th century the Concordat converted it into a parish church.

This distinctive church lies at some 3 km from Santiago and is surrounded by the charming verdure of the countryside. It comprises a basilican ground-plan with nave and two nave-aisles, barrel vaults and elegant semicircular apses that contrast with the robust 18th-century buttresses. The interior constitutes a perfect sample of the Romanesque style of the 12th century. The 13th- and 14th- century tombs placed along the walls of the church are of particular interest, as also the Romanesque cloister — one of the most beautiful in Galicia.

The unusual inclination of the columns, arches and vaults arouses great interest. Some experts state that it conforms to the builders' bold plans, but others consider that the slant is due to a technical error.

THE UNIVERSITY

The University was founded in 1501; originally it occupied a building in the Rúa Nueva. Later, thanks to the efforts of the third Bishop Fonseca, the entity that had been founded with the name *Estudio Viejo* attained a standing of some prestige, which was increased when the University passed into royal patronage during the reign of Philip II; the institution became dependent on the state as from the middle of the 19th century.

The University now occupies a magnificent stone building on the site of the Society of Jesus' old Novitiate. Building work began in 1769 — following plans by the architect Melchor de Prado, later revised by Ventura Rodríguez and Pérez Machado — and concluded in 1805. A further storey was added later (1894-1904) and the group of statues by Ferreiro — a depiction of Minerva — was removed and replaced by statues of the University's founders, by Ramón Núñez, in the modern frieze.

The departments of the University of Compostela installed in this central building are: the rector's office (with the magnificent 17th-century choir-stalls from Osera monastery), the central hall decorated with frescoes by Fenollera and González; and the libraries, Archives (conserving numerous manuscripts and some five hundred volumes containing official documents) and Faculties of Law and Philosophy & Arts.

The libraries are of great importance: the University Library, which has about a hundred incunabula and the Polyglot Bibles of Alcalá and Antwerp; the Lago González Library, some 6,000 volumes; the America Library, and the Philosophy & Arts Library.

Santiago University: the sumptuous central hall.

Santiago University: the spacious rector's hall.

THE CITY

Four elements are fundamental in penetrating the spirit of Compostela and reaching an appreciable understanding of the city: the surrounding countryside, the rain, the noble carved stone (Romanesque, plateresque or baroque) and the character of the people.

The polychromatic landscape, dominated by an amazing green, rich in shades, which seems to bore amorously into the entrails of the earth, here and there crowns the city's skyline. The countryside makes its presence felt in the city, slipping in by the bustling *rúas* (streets), from the paradisiacal rural views glimpsed from El Obradoiro that may be con-templated from the beautiful Herradura avenue or around the streets running from the Plaza de Vigo to the Puerta del Camino, by the *Cuesta* ("slope") *de Santo Domingo* and at the source of the enchanting Rúa de San Pedro, with its picturesque houses with attractive chimneys. In a fine poem from his magnificent book *Con pólvora y magnolias,* Méndez-Ferrín evokes this ambivalent country/city condition that is characteristic of Santiago:

En Compostela pode un home
escollar óboe e docísimo cor ao contrapeso,
decair nos tremedoiros
(vibra, corazón gastado),
tenra especie de prantas espiráis

e añuca ou seixo de xogar entre os dedos.
Pode pedra luída
alzarte sobre sí coma un querreiro
é proclamado rei de oucas e carballeiras vellas.
En Compostela pode un vento duro
estremecer o corazón da Europa campesina
que todos temos dentro sin decilo.

Rain is always a possibility in Santiago. It makes the artistic, time-honoured stones of the monuments shine and imparts a fantastic iridescence to the winding roadways in the romantic nights of Santiago. The Rúa del Villar or the Rúa Nueva, seen from their characteristic, welcoming colonnades on a rainy night, offer a fascinating aesthetic image. García Lorca lauded — in surprisingly accurate Galician — the beauty of rain in Compostela by night:

Chove en Santiago
na noite escura.
Herbas de prata e de sono
cobren a valeira rúa.

The artistically-carved stone (essentially Romanesque, also baroque and, to a lesser extent, plateresque) is apparent at any street corner and stimulates aesthetic reactions the length and breadth of the city, from the Rúa Nueva to the Quintana de los Muertos,

A beautiful back-lighting effect in the poetical framework of the Plaza del Obradoiro.

from Las Platerías to El Obradoiro, from the *Cuesta de Santo Domingo* or La Herredura to the site, in the middle of the countryside, of the Collegiate Church of Santa María la Real del Sar. This is the charming stone of Compostela, sung in superb verses by the poet Salvador García-Bodaño in *Tempo de Compostela:*

> *E frutos de pedra derramábanse*
> *polos muros dos pazos*
> *e das igrexas...*
> *A tarde era o adro da calma*
> *nas quintanas do sono*
> *e o cantar da i-auga*
> *brincaba das gorgazas*
> *soando e resoando*
> *nos recantos do tempo nas calexas.*

Santiago having become the real religious and intellectual capital of Galicia, the Cathedral and the University seem to have left a subtle stamp on the character of the people. The inhabitants have a lively sense of humour — an unmistakable sign of a distinguished spirit — and characteristically behave with restraint and courtesy. The considerable student population fills the streets of Compostela with youth and happiness. Their presence is particularly apparent in the evening, from seven o'clock to half past ten, in the Calle del Franco and surrounding streets. One can barely make one's way along the pavements, which are flanked by the tempting windows of an infinite number of bars and restaurants. During this period, the Calle del Franco is swarming, a hive of people, of whom the evident majority are students. Suddenly, around half past ten, when one has scarcely had time to take in this popular phenomenon, the streets and bars are emptied, as if by magic. The students' sacred supper-time has come...

Otero Pedrayo wrote an admirable description of the city: ''The presence, sensation and enjoyment of the spirit of the West — this is not the least of the prodigies offered to the traveller in Santiago. The vessel bound for high places seems to await the eternal journey in the cloisters and colonnades; silence, rhythmically measured by the peals from the bell-tower, accompanies the flight of the river of time towards the brink of immortality. One should not — cannot — look in Compostela for banal joys nor for the pulsing reflexes of big cities. The self-same capacity of resonance demonstrated in the solemn moments of its art shows that only matters of essence, of grandeur, are worthy of this environment. Santiago has an exceptional fate that avoids at all stages the danger, the reiterated temptation, of all that is vulgar, copied, standard.''

Santiago is a city made to measure for human beings. Spiritual questions predominate here, and the individual does not feel hemmed in by the absurd haste that suffocates the vital process in today's world. Even the most trivial aspect acquires warmth and a style of its own in Compostela, such as the unforgettable spectacle offered for decades by ''the three Maries' '' classic promenade: three sisters (only one is still alive, Coralia Fandiño Richard), who used to stroll down Calle del Franco or La Alameda, meticulously dressed and made up despite their advanced age; or the extraordinary *tertulia* (regular informal gathering) in the ''Derby'' bar, attended by students, teachers, writers, journalists, painters, politicians....

Façade of the Faculty of Medicine, and San Francisco church.

Plateresque front of the old Colegio Mayor de Fonseca.

Charming close-up of the beautiful Fonseca cloister. ▷

COLEGIO DE FONSECA

The Fonseca dynasty is closely linked to the history of Santiago. There were three archbishops of this surname: Alonso de Fonseca I, who brought peace to the archdiocese, Alonso de Fonseca II (who protagonised a confrontation with Pedro Madruga, participated actively in controlling the revolution of the *irmandiños* and took the side of Isabella *la Católica*) and Alonso de Fonseca III. The latter became Archbishop of Toledo; under his mandate the *Cortes* or parliament met in San Francisco monastery in Santiago, presided over by Charles I, in 1520.

The third Fonseca was the founder of the College (*Colegio Mayor*) that bears his name and also that of Santiago Alfeo. The building stands at one end of the popular Calle del Franco; it was built from 1532 to 1544. It is a beautiful monument, in the plateresque style, built under the supervision of the master craftsmen Alonso de Gontin and Jácome García, following designs by the architects Juan de Alava and Alonso de Covarrubias. There is a beautiful doorway and an elegant tower. The fine cloister, previously a *Colegio Menor,* now houses the Faculty of Pharmacy. The former Fonseca College extends as far as El Obradoiro, making up an architectural ensemble with the edifice occupied by the *Seminario de Estudios Gallegos* (College of Galician Studies) and the contiguous *Colegio de San Jerónimo,* which displays a superb Romanesque doorway.

The door of the Pharmacy Faculty, in Fonseca College.

Palacio de Rajoy: *neo-classical façade.*

"HOSTAL DE LOS REYES CATÓLICOS" AND "PALACIO DE RAJOY"

Previously a hospice for pilgrims founded by the Catholic Monarchs, Ferdinand and Isabella, at the request of Dean Don Diego de Muros, the *Hostal de los Reyes Católicos* has since 1954 been one of the most spacious, sumptuous and comfortable hotels in Europe. The building occupies an area of some 5,000 sq.m and was classified as a national monument in 1912. It stands in the Plaza del Obradoiro, to the right of the Cathedral. The building works of this grand edifice (which for several centuries had the function of a Royal Hospital) began in 1501 and concluded in 1511; the plans were by Enrique de Egas, although other elements, in late Gothic, Renaissance and Baro-

que styles, were later incorporated into its original architecture.

The former Royal Hospital comprises four courtyards distributed around the church and has three majestic stone façades. The fine plateresque front displays artistic statues on either side, a pair of imperial coats of arms and two large, symmetrical windows. The church is sumptuously decorated: the extraordinary beauty of its Gothic altars and the exquisite screen in the chapel are outstanding. The famous *Salón Real* ("Royal Hall"), presided over by portraits of the Catholic Monarchs, is powerfully attractive by virtue of its lavish ornamentation. From one of the building's windows Philip II watched a bull-fight held in the Plaza del Obradoiro.

The Rajoy mansion, now the seat of the civic authorities, stands opposite the cathedral's baroque

Main front of the Palacio de Bendaña, *in Plaza del Toral.*

Church of Santa María Salomé: Romanesque porch. ▷

façade in the Plaza del Obradoiro, to the right of the *Hostal de los Reyes Católicos.* The vast building, designed by Charles Lemaur, a Frenchman, was constructed from 1766 to 1772. The main front is supported by a granite colonnade with fourteen round arches. In the central part the outstanding items include a beautiful portico of five monumental columns, and the section of six Ionic columns crowned by a pediment with, above, an equestrian statue of the Apostle by Ferreiro. The building's grandness and its architectural profile are in perfect harmony with the impressive Plaza del Obradoiro, the incomparable square that also embraces the façades of the Cathedral, the *Hostal,* the old *Colegio de San Jerónimo* and the Archbishops' Palace.

SANTA MARIA SALOME CHURCH

This church was founded in the 12th century; its enchantingly beautiful structure — Romanesque doorway protected by a 15th-century ogive porch, and a baroque tower — stands out surprisingly among the colonnades, crowded with passers-by, of the Rúa Nueva. The keystone of the porch over the Romanesque doorway displays an image of the Virgin, seated, flanked by figures of the Annunciation.

The baroque tower, the work of José Crespo, dates from 1743. Inside the church, one should highlight the ogive vaulting of the chapels of Christ and of S Joseph, the altar-piece by Miguel de Romay and the 18th-century Calvary by Bartolomé Fernández.

Façade of the Seminario Mayor *(seminary).*

QUINTANA DE LOS MUERTOS

This beautiful square was previously a cemetery; the *Puerta Santa* ("Holy Door") of the Cathedral gives onto it. The baroque silhouette of the *Casa de la Parra* ("Vine House") stands at the top of a stairway, to the north of the square; to the east is the massive monastery of San Payo de Antealtares with, in the centre section of its façade, a stone tablet commemorating the swearing-in of the "Galician Literary Batallion," made up of students who fought against the troops of Napoleon. According to legend, a medical student fell from one of the convent's window-grilles when trying to abduct a novice nun

with whom he was in love. The square constitutes an ideal setting for the celebration of open-air festivities; on summer nights sizable groups of young people congregate there to sing, drink a bottle of wine or simply to converse and enjoy the cool air.

After giving suitable praise to Las Platerías, Otero Pedrayo describes the broad square in these terms: "This lake of silence, of memories, enclosed by the walls — of bare or carved stone — of the Quintana, displays the same religious nature, almost ascetic at certain times of day, though not without the noble quality of life in Galicia in times past. It is to the east of the basilica, and although the ecstatic beauty of the Romanesque apses does not actually give onto the square, it is decorated by an orderly line of styliz-

◁ *A superb panorama of Santiago de Compostela.*

ed ornaments, figures of cypress-trees and baroque canapés above the *Puerta Santa,* like a garden in stone; it is also ennobled by the great doorway called the *Puerta Real* ('Royal Door'), of balanced lines and classical composition."

San Payo de Antealtares monastery was founded by Alfonso II. The monks of the time guarded the tomb of the Apostle, to whom the monastery was dedicated until the 12th century. San Pedro de Mezonzo was one of the abbots: he became Bishop of Santiago and is attributed the authorship of the *Salve Regina.* The architectural structure of San Payo that we see today dates from the 17th-18th centuries. The church, built by Fray Gabriel Casas, was consecrated in 1707; according to the tradition, its marble altar stone was placed over the Apostle's tomb by his disciples and consecrated for the sacrifice of Mass.

The *Casa de la Parra* ("Vine House") is a secular building in the Quintana de los Muertos that draws one's attention powerfully, for the artistic elegance characterizing its architecture; baroque in style, it displays a superb chimney.

The graceful front of the Casa de la Parra *("Vine House").*

Fine ogive arches at the Monastery of San Francisco de Valdediós.

Monastery of San Martín Pinario: vault of the refectory.

Cloister of the old San Clemente College.

COLEGIO DE SAN CLEMENTE

This college was founded by Archbishop Don Juan de Sanclemente Torquemada in 1602; as Otero Pedrayo says, it was originally intended for "18 students (this number was never reached) having passed the *Bachiller* or school-leaving examination, thus called *Pasantes;* coming from Galicia or Córdoba, since the founder was from the latter province, or from one of the dioceses that paid the *Voto de Santiago"* — a tribute of wheat or bread. In 1829 it was the seat of the "Economic Association of Friends of the Country" and housed an interesting museum and a library of some ten thousand volumes. The former San Clemente College building, which has a balanced façade and spacious cloister, stands by the Alameda and is now a girls' school.

ROSALIA DE CASTRO'S HOUSE AND MUSEUM

The house called La Matanza, where the authoress of *Follas Novas* was born, has been converted into the Rosalía de Castro Museum. It is located in Padrón — some 20 km from Santiago — by the side of Iria-Flavia, where the writer Camilo José Cela was born. The building is a spacious edifice in the characteristic

The kitchen at La Matanza, the house where Rosalía de Castro lived.

rural Galician style. The galleries house many articles and pieces of furniture (including the bed) that belonged to Rosalía, as well as a large number of books and documents relating to the life and work of the genial poetess of Galicia.

Contemplation of La Matanza seems to provoke the melancholy that so enchantingly permeates Rosalía de Castro's verses:

Airiños, airiños aires,
airiños da miña terra;
airiños, airiños aires;
airiños, levaime a ela.
Sin ela vivir non podo,
non podo vivir contenta,
qu'a donde queira que vaia,
cróbeme unha sombra espesa.

The room where Rosalía de Castro died: hers was the most profound, moving poetic voice of the lands of Galicia.

A view of La Matanza, on the outskirts of Padrón, now the House and Museum devoted to the authoress of Cantares Gallegos and Follas Novas.

THE ALAMEDA AND SANTA SUSANA

The horseshoe-shaped La Alameda promenade is one of the most fascinating, popular and characteristic parts of Santiago. It spreads around the Santa Susana enclosure, which is planted with large, ancient oak-trees and is the hillock known in the 11th century as *altarium pullorum.* As Otero Pedrayo says, the Alameda is composed of ''three salons, in accordance with 19th-century etiquette (which in this respect was very 18th-century): the one in the centre for the nobility, the right-hand salon for the common people, and the one on the left reserved for elderly clerics and professors; all this without pragmatism, due to the imperatives of custom... It has lost some of its old trees but in their place, along with the white and pink Camellia, flourishes the tree that characteristically adorns Galician country houses: the tree that sheds a carpet of colourful, fleshy, cold petals on the ground in the gardens in April, as if bemoaning the flight of the pale suns of winter.''

People now stroll in the three salons of the Alameda without class distinctions. The *Herradura* (''Horseshoe'') is entirely popular, without having lost an iota of its natural beauty and distinction. Courting couples go there to find complicity for their love in the verdure and enjoy (as Méndez-Ferrín says in a very beautiful poem entitled *Diante de Compostela doutros días*) ''very long kisses among the roses of the Horseshoe.''

The popular, romantic scene is nostalgically evoked by another poet, Salvador García-Bodaño:

> *Aquelas mañáns de música*
> *na Alameda*
> *nunha ida e volta de adeuses*
> *polo paseo...*
> *   As xentes do pobo*
> *   na varanda dos domingos.*
> *A primeira moza*
> *e os primeiros soños*
> *no inxenuo banco*
> *de tantas agardas.*

Night-time view of the cathedral from the vantage-point
of La Herradura.

Quén ten
o retrato do minuto
co rebulicio daquelas horas
nas láminas do aire?

Three statues stand in the shade of ancient trees in
the Alameda: they depict Rosalía de Castro (by the
sculptor Clivilles, unveiled on July 30th, 1917), Ad-
miral Méndez Núñez and the archbishop of Laodicea
(now Letica).

From the Paseo de la Herredura one can enjoy a
broad, beautiful view of the countryside surrounding
the city, and also fascinating perspectives of Santiago
itself, dominated by the lofty spires of the cathedral.
The Paseo de Bóveda runs west from the Herredura
avenue, then the Students' Residence gardens and
San Lorenzo wood appear, and the pine-trees that
climb the foothills of El Pedroso... The statue of
Manuel Ventura Figueroa, sculptured by Vidal in the
late 19th century, is in this area; the modern architectural profile of the Science Faculty and the
Astronomy Observatory — with a Minerva carved by
Ferreiro — stand to the left.

The church of Santa Susana is situated on the hill of
the same name, in the middle of the Paseo de la Herradura. The original church was demolished by
Gelmírez so as to build on its site the present-day
fabric, consecrated — as Otero Pedrayo wrote — to
"the Saint whose body was, with other holy bodies,
brought from Braga." The church, comprising a
single nave without aisles, was rebuilt at the begin-
ning of the 18th century; its humble presence at the
top of the hill would seem to invite us to recall its
Romanesque origins.

Fascinating juxtaposition of the countryside and the cathedral spires.

FOLKLORE AND CRAFT WORK

Of all the *fiestas* celebrated in Compostela, the most outstanding are in honour of the Apostle. These begin on July 15th and continue until the 31st. On the most important day of the festivities, July 25th (now also the "National Day of Galicia"), the city is invaded by pilgrims who come from the furthest lands of Galicia and from further still. The ambience reaches a high point and the commemoration of S James the Apostle's Day becomes an event of universal significance when the 25th is a Sunday, that is, in Holy Years.

Despite its considerable dimensions, the Plaza del Obradoiro is then barely large enough to accommodate the thousands and thousands of people who flock to Santiago to participate in the traditional dances and to watch the different manifestations of Galician folklore. They dance *muiñeiras* on the old paving-stones of the square; sweet *alalás* and manly *aturuxos* resound in the warm night air. The bagpipes play incessant melodies of a charming Celtic flavour as background music, while the cheerful tambourines superimpose their strange tones. The whole city is full of bustle and joy: it seems to relive the Dionysiac passion that, permeated with religiousness, is constantly present in the Romanesque style.

A solemn religious service is celebrated in the cathedral on the 25th. The archbishop presides over a grand procession, accompanied by the bishops of several other cities and the members of the Chapter. The relic of S James is carried on people's shoulders and the *botafumeiro* (censer) swings like a pendulum from one side of the transept to the other, propelled

by eight men skilfully operating as many ropes. The interior of the church is impregnated with the perfumed smoke of incense. After the solemn mass, when the strokes of midday resound from the bell-tower, the *Gigantes y Cabezudos* (carnival figures of giants and others with enormous heads) leave the cathedral by the *Puerta Santa* in La Quintana; there they dance, surrounded by the crowd, to the sound of squibs and rockets. The festive parade then proceeds from La Quintana to Las Platerías, presided over by "Coca" and "Coco," a popular couple got up in picturesque dress following the latest fashion: nowadays they depict tourists.

On the eve of S James' Day the crowds assembled in the Plaza del Obradoiro watch the burning of the "Apostle's Fire" — a castle of fireworks with Moorish traits — in front of the cathedral's baroque façade.

The *fiestas* celebrating the Day of the Apostle go back to 1508; they began with the dance of the Giants in La Quintana when the City Hall clock struck twelve. The joyful procession — presided over by the Mayor and Justice of the city, riding on a mule — wound through the streets of Compostela, packed with pilgrims; many of them were foreigners, French and Germans in particular.

Other famous festivities in Santiago include those of S John and the *fiesta* held in Belvis on Easter Monday, in honour of S Peter the Martyr; but the Easter and Corpus Christi celebrations pale into insignificance when compared with the splendour of those held on the Apostle James' Day.

Important international competitions in the sphere of music are organized in Santiago de Compostela nowadays. The International Summer Courses and the exhibitions sponsored by the Institute of Galician Studies are also of undoubtable interest.

Santiago has a productive industry in the manufacture of craft objects, such as pilgrims' scallops, figures of the patron saint, reproductions of the *botafumeiro* and other souvenirs connected with S James.

Children, wearing Galician clothes, in front of a stone cross.

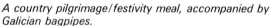

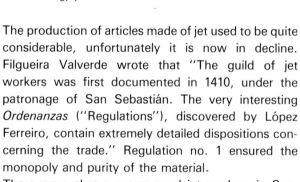

A country pilgrimage/festivity meal, accompanied by Galician bagpipes.

A Galician girl carrying a raxo *pie on her head.*

The production of articles made of jet used to be quite considerable, unfortunately it is now in decline. Filgueira Valverde wrote that "The guild of jet workers was first documented in 1410, under the patronage of San Sebastián. The very interesting *Ordenanzas* ("Regulations"), discovered by López Ferreiro, contain extremely detailed dispositions concerning the trade." Regulation no. 1 ensured the monopoly and purity of the material.

There were always many good jet workers in Santiago. An idea of the importance reached by these skilful craftsmen's guild may be drawn from the fact that one of the cathedral's façades *(Fachada de la Azabachería)* is named after them. There are still admirable artisans who fashion delicate jet pieces, in particular the "higa" (fig), an amulet against the *meigallo* or evil eye, which represents a clenched fist with the thumb projecting between the index and middle fingers; the scallop shell; or the open hand, a gesture of generosity in contrast with the *figa* ("higa"), which is of a defensive or insulting nature; also images of the Apostle and rings mounted in silver. Pontevedra Museum conserves interesting mediaeval jet pieces by jewellers from Santiago.

Santiago led the field in the rocket-making profession from the 16th century onwards. Also, there were always abundant *picheleiros* — makers of pewter tankards — who even had a guild of their own.

GASTRONOMY

All the cities in Galicia have the reputation of delicious cooking; Santiago is one of those with the best and most varied cuisine. The city being surrounded by fertile countryside, and given the proximity to the coastline of the *Rías Bajas* — as beautiful as it is rich in first-class fish and seafood — Compostela benefits from the best meat, the most delicious vegetables, exquisite fruit and the tastiest cheeses from the Ulla valley and the stone-walled fields of Monterroso and Palas de Rey; as also *lacones* (shoulders of pork) from Sarria, the renowned *chorizo* (salami) from Villalba and the finest varieties of fish and exquisite seafood from the Atlantic.

With regard to wines, Otero Pedrayo says that ''In times gone by the best wine in Galicia was drunk in Compostela, he (the inhabitant of Santiago) is a refined, critical drinker with a demanding palate. In the classic days of the nobility only fine, white wine appeared on aristocratic tables. As authorities we would cite some passages of the 'Codex of Callisto' and the

The hórreo — granary — and a farmer's cart, characteristic of the countryside of Galicia.

Seafood: the glory of Santiago's restaurants.

A pie, octopus, scallops, nécoras, *crab....* ▷

Historia Compostelana, with copious lists of the supplies that entered the city, more or less the same as those that come nowadays. The taste and pleasure of sumptuous, slow banquets shine through certain passages of the Gelmírez Chronicle. The brackets of the dining hall in the Archbishops' Palace bear carvings of the beautiful, heraldic *empanadas* (pies) of Compostela, so as to arouse today's appetite with the memories of those past.''

Outstanding, unforgettable dishes of Santiago's cuisine are the pies of lamprey, eels, cockles or black wrasse, made with the excellent wheat bread from Deza and La Mahía. The pies of maize bread are also highly appreciated, especially those containing cockles or cod. Lamprey from the river Ulla stewed in the Bordeaux style, a princely dish, graces the tables of the best restaurants in Compostela from February to April. Dishes that are always present in the memory of the refined palates of Santiago include shoulder of pork with turnip shoots *(lacón con grelos)*, the omelettes (of ham, asparagus, brains or potato and *chorizo*), hake (roasted or cooked in a *caldeirada*), turbot grilled or cooked in "green sauce," conger eel in pies or "green sauce" and — in June — sardines baked with *cachelos* (meat, potatoes and peppers). Tripe with chickpeas and octopus *ó estilo feira* are two very typical dishes in Santiago; the latter is cooked — in a copper pot, if possible — and dressed with salt, paprika and raw olive oil.

The granary at Carnota, considered to be the largest in Galicia.

A bucolic image in the environs of Redondela. ▷

A stranger contemplating the tempting window-displays of the restaurants in Calle del Franco might well conclude that Santiago is the shellfish centre of Galicia. The whole complex, fascinating gastronomical world of Galician seafood is present in the city of the Apostle: from *percebes* (barnacles), fit for a cardinal, whose delicate flavour is unlike any other, to scallops, the *venera* of S James; also the tasty, lowly cockles, exquisite oysters from the Ría de Arosa, raw or steamed clams, prawns, the very fine *nécoras,* delicious crab, large and small lobsters, Norway lobster and the reasonably-priced mussels.

The wines merit a paragraph of their own. The climate of Santiago favours Galicia's good wine, which is not strong in alcohol but has an exquisite taste. In Compostela one can always accompany meals based on fish and/or shellfish with wines of quality such as Albariño, Ribeiro or Condado. The acidic little wine from the Ulla is not a poor match for these dishes, either. If the meal is of meat, the most advisable red wines are Ribeiro, Barrantes or, if possible, the wine from Amandi that apparently pleased Augustus's palate 2,000 years ago.

For sweets, mention should be made of *tarta santiaguesa, leche frita* (fried milk), the *empiñonados* (cakes with pine kernels) from Belvis, biscuits from Compostela, rice pudding, local cheeses and fresh Galician fruit.

Contents

Collection ALL EUROPE

	Spanish	French	English	German	Italian	Catalan	Dutch	Swedish	Portuguese	Japanese	Finnish
1 ANDORRA	•										
2 LISBON	•										
3 LONDON	•										
4 BRUGES	•										
5 PARIS	•										
6 MONACO	•										
7 VIENNA	•										
11 VERDUN	•										
12 THE TOWER OF LONDON	•										
13 ANTWERP	•										
14 WESTMINSTER ABBEY	•										
15 THE SPANISH RIDING SCHOOL IN VIENNA	•										
16 FATIMA	•										
17 WINDSOR CASTLE	•										
19 COTE D'AZUR	•										
22 BRUSSELS	•										
23 SCHÖNBRUNN PALACE	•										
24 ROUTE OF PORT WINE	•										
26 HOFBURG PALACE	•										
27 ALSACE	•										
31 MALTA											
32 PERPIGNAN											
33 STRASBOURG	•										
35 CERDAGNE - CAPCIR											

Collection ART IN SPAIN

	Spanish	French	English	German	Italian	Catalan	Dutch	Swedish	Portuguese	Japanese	Finnish
1 PALAU DE LA MUSICA CATALANA	•		•			•					
2 GAUDI	•	•	•	•	•					•	
3 PRADO MUSEUM I (Spanish Painting)	•	•	•	•	•					•	
4 PRADO MUSEUM II (Foreign Painting)	•	•	•	•	•						
5 MONASTERY OF GUADALUPE	•										
6 THE CASTLE OF XAVIER	•	•	•	•						•	
7 THE FINE ARTS MUSEUM OF SEVILLE	•	•	•	•	•						
8 SPANISH CASTLES	•	•	•	•							
9 THE CATHEDRALS OF SPAIN	•	•	•	•							
10 THE CATHEDRAL OF GERONA	•	•	•								
14 PICASSO	•	•	•	•	•					•	
15 REALES ALCAZARES (ROYAL PALACE OF SEVILLE)	•	•	•	•	•						
16 MADRID'S ROYAL PALACE	•	•	•	•	•						
17 ROYAL MONASTERY OF EL ESCORIAL	•	•	•	•	•						
18 THE WINES OF CATALONIA	•										
19 THE ALHAMBRA AND THE GENERALIFE	•	•	•	•	•						
20 GRANADA AND THE ALHAMBRA	•	•	•	•	•						
21 ROYAL ESTATE OF ARANJUEZ	•	•	•	•	•						
22 ROYAL ESTATE OF EL PARDO	•	•	•	•	•						
23 ROYAL HOUSES	•	•	•	•	•						
24 ROYAL PALACE OF SAN ILDEFONSO	•	•	•	•	•						
25 HOLY CROSS OF THE VALLE DE LOS CAIDOS	•	•	•	•	•						
26 OUR LADY OF THE PILLAR OF SARAGOSSA	•	•	•	•							
28 POBLET ABTEI	•	•	•	•	•						

Collection ALL SPAIN

	Spanish	French	English	German	Italian	Catalan	Dutch	Swedish	Portuguese	Japanese	Finnish
1 ALL MADRID	•	•	•	•	•				•		
2 ALL BARCELONA	•	•	•	•	•	•					
3 ALL SEVILLE	•	•	•	•	•				•		
4 ALL MAJORCA	•	•	•	•	•						
5 ALL THE COSTA BRAVA	•	•	•	•	•						
6 ALL MALAGA and the Costa del Sol	•	•	•	•	•		•				
7 ALL THE CANARY ISLANDS (Gran Canaria)	•	•	•	•	•		•	•			
8 ALL CORDOBA	•	•	•	•	•				•		
9 ALL GRANADA	•	•	•	•	•		•		•		
10 ALL VALENCIA	•	•	•	•	•						
11 ALL TOLEDO	•	•	•	•	•				•		
12 ALL SANTIAGO	•	•	•	•	•						
13 ALL IBIZA and Formentera	•	•	•	•	•						
14 ALL CADIZ and the Costa de la Luz	•	•	•	•	•						
15 ALL MONTSERRAT	•	•	•	•	•	•					
16 ALL SANTANDER and Cantabria	•	•	•	•							
17 ALL THE CANARY ISLANDS II, (Tenerife)	•	•	•	•	•		•	•			•
20 ALL BURGOS	•	•	•	•	•						
21 ALL ALICANTE and the Costa Blanca	•	•	•	•	•		•				
22 ALL NAVARRA	•	•	•	•							
23 ALL LERIDA	•	•	•	•		•					
24 ALL SEGOVIA	•	•	•	•	•						
25 ALL SARAGOSSA	•	•	•	•	•						
26 ALL SALAMANCA	•	•	•	•				•			
27 ALL AVILA	•	•	•	•	•						
28 ALL MINORCA	•	•	•	•							
29 ALL SAN SEBASTIAN and Guipúzcoa	•	•									
30 ALL ASTURIAS	•										
31 ALL LA CORUNNA and the Rías Altas	•	•	•								
32 ALL TARRAGONAe	•	•	•								
33 ALL MURCIAe	•	•	•	•							
34 ALL VALLADOLIDe	•	•	•								
35 ALL GIRONAe	•	•	•								
36 ALL HUESCAe	•	•									
37 ALL JAENe	•	•	•								
38 ALL ALMERIAe	•	•	•								
40 ALL CUENCAe	•	•	•								
41 ALL LEONe	•	•	•								
42 ALL PONTEVEDRA, VIGO and the Rías Bajas	•	•	•								
43 ALL RONDA	•	•	•	•	•						
44 ALL SORIA	•										
46 ALL EXTREMADURA	•										
47 ALL ANDALUSIA	•	•	•	•	•		•				
52 ALL MORELLA	•	•	•		•						

Collection ALL AMERICA

	Spanish	French	English	German	Italian	Catalan	Dutch	Swedish	Portuguese	Japanese	Finnish
1 PUERTO RICO	•		•								
2 SANTO DOMINGO	•										
3 QUEBEC		•	•								
4 COSTA RICA	•										

Collection ALL AFRICA

	Spanish	French	English	German	Italian	Catalan	Dutch	Swedish	Portuguese	Japanese	Finnish
1 MOROCCO	•	•	•	•							
2 THE SOUTH OF MOROCCO	•	•	•	•							
3 TUNISIA		•	•	•	•						
4 RWANDA		•